brown's guide
to the good life

brown's guide

david brown

to the good life

without tears, fears or boredom

barricade books • fort lee, new jersey

NOTE: Three chapters of this book were based on articles that have appeared in *Town and Country* and *Variety*.

Published by Barricade Books Inc.
185 Bridge Plaza North
Suite 308-A
Fort Lee, NJ 07024

www.barricadebooks.com

Library of Congress Cataloging-in-Publication Data
A copy of this title's Library of Congress Cataloging-in-Publication
Data is available on request from the Library of Congress.

ISBN 1-56980-282-3

Designed by Pauline Neuwirth

First Printing
Manufactured in the United States of America

contents

oh god, another book!

i believe many people have a book to write. Mercifully, they don't write it—energy or confidence lacking. My reason for the one you hold is that I've lived through remarkable times. I watched Charles Lindbergh take off on his no-frills 33½-hour flight to Paris in 1927, and I've flown the same route in 2002 in two hours and 57 minutes aboard the Concorde, champagne and caviar in hand. This is not an aviation tome but rather about flying high through life, experiencing daunting crashes, exhilarating updrafts and happy landings.

In the midst of this hubris, I've learned some things about life. These include pain, gain, sorrows and how to negotiate through fortune's shoals. Some of my conclusions may help you avoid the rocks and shallows—though I hasten to add that this is not an industrial strength self-help book.

Consider my words the musings of a geezer (89) who has experienced the worst and best and can possibly spare you the former and guide you to the latter.

DAVID BROWN

JANUARY 2006

NEW YORK CITY

brown's guide
to the good life

1. secrets of success and failure

success is . . .
  The love of a good woman (or man)
  Health
  Enough money not to have to do what you loathe
  Work that is its own reward (you'd almost do it for
    nothing)
  A Monte Cristo cigar (Havana, of course) after a
    sumptuous dinner
  The love and respect of children
  Death without pain (preferably while sleeping)
  Accomplishing one thing of which you're proud
  Living without regrets or anger

  I don't know who said this but you are successful if
you feel good about yourself and you are a failure if you
feel rotten about yourself, no matter how much money
you possess. Achieving success in any field requires a pos-
itive attitude. It also requires an ability to surmount

disappointments and setbacks—by trying again and again to reach your goals.

The secret of failure is:

My beloved friend, Pamela Hedley, says: "The capacity for self delusion is infinite." *Ja wohl.*

However talented, those who berate or persecute others cannot succeed.

Living through lies. Falsehood may provide a short term advantage but the end game is always failure.

Making your life–style more important than your ability to support it can lead to insolvency and even larceny and jail time.

Here is an assortment of things to avoid:

Putting off difficult decisions.

Failing to act decisively.

Not keeping promises. Broken promises cause broken careers.

Punctuality problems. Not being on time is a bore. Late comers are never late (or early) bloomers.

Rigidity. Things change. Life changes. Times change. Those who cannot bend with the winds of change are destined to break. Addiction to a single point of view when it becomes untenable is a terminal trait.

Failure to take risks. Life's lessons always come from

studying and learning from mistakes. Bounce like a ball.

Ignorance through lack of curiosity. One must read obsessively. It is a gratifying substitute for experience.

2. musings on the road to 90

it's not true that the rest of life is the best of life. You've outlived your doctors and maybe a wife or two— even a child. You ache, you stagger, you repeat yourself and even then you can't remember what you said.

But, as some wiseacre said, consider the alternative. If fate has spared you a stroke, a heart attack or a malignancy, you still have some delights to enjoy.

Reading is one of them—better than watching DVDs, movies, TV or sportcasts. Sex, even in the age of Viagra and Cialis is problematic, to put it charitably. Apologies to the source for not remembering, but the wife of an aging Lothario is credited with saying, "I thought the legs gave out first."

Indeed, legs do give out. When you need to hold the arms of your chair to push yourself up, you've reached the age of immobility. Walking may become an ordeal and staircases a challenge. Elevators and escalators are your new best friends.

So are memories. Instead of counting sheep or former lovers, I visit my departed friends in order to lull myself to sleep. I see them—and me—in the flower of our youth, full of vitality, optimism and requited love for each other. Then, alas, I wake up to evacuate my bladder and my dreams.

Avoid settling scores. It is a waste of time or energy. Instead keep score.

A little booze sometimes helps, unless you're the addictive type. It cleans out the arteries and makes you seem more amusing than you are. (Some may disagree.)

Morning brings the newspapers and I turn quickly not to page one but to my personal sports page—the obituaries. These announce the latest losers in the game of life.

Advice? The best I've heard was from actress Barbara Stanwyck who was quoted in William Safire and Leonard Safire's book, *Good Advice*. Miss Stanwyck counseled: "Know when your time is up. It's the only advice I have. Hell, I knew twenty-five years ago it wasn't going to last. Sooner or later, the demand won't be there, and you better get ready for it. I know actresses who go ape if they're not invited to a party. What the hell is that? I am content. Happiness is within yourself. Get ready for the dream to fade. If I'm no longer in demand, so what?

"I see no reason to go into a decline or hit the bottle

or sink into a melancholy depression. I've had my time and it was lovely. And I'm very grateful for it. But now I'll move over and make room for somebody else."

Notwithstanding Miss Stanwyck's advice, I'll keep working if they let me. Retirement is a drag. Work is the best preventative against Alzheimer's disease and premature death. (All death is premature in my opinion.)

If you're as lucky as I am, you'll have a companion to see you through the grungy years. In a scene from Eugene O'Neil's *Ah, Wilderness!* an elderly couple are enjoying a summer night on the porch. "I can only remember a few nights that were are beautiful as this," the man says, "and they were long ago when your mother and I were young . . . Yet ah that spring should vanish with the Rose. Well spring isn't everything is it, Essie. There's a lot to be said for autumn. That's got beauty too. And winter—if you're together." Even at 90.

The late, great Jewish comedian Myron Cohen told of a rich, elderly man smitten by a much younger woman. Insecure because of their age difference, he hesitantly inquired, "If I lost all my money, would you still love me?" "Of course I would," purred the young beauty, "and I'd miss you."

Without money, one may miss a great deal more than a hustling young woman. Lacking are the sweet feeling of financial independence, the wherewithal to escape tyrannical bosses and wretched jobs. A little (or a lot) of filthy lucre can assure one the ability to work, travel, dine and live as one pleases.

If you would aspire to this blessed state, you need not be rich. What you must do is spend less than you earn. To paraphrase Charles Dickens: "Income $10,000. Expenses $9,000. Happiness. Income $10,000, Expenses $10,500. Misery."

My mother was able to be independent on an income from investments of $1,600 a year. On her $1,600 annual income she was even able to save money enough to bail me out occasionally. True, those were early times when a dollar was a dollar but the principle applies.

When I met my wife she was saving $100 a week out of her $300 a week salary. This was enough to lend money to me, a highly paid film executive who knew how to make money but not how to keep it. I was an economic illiterate.

Don't you be one.

I never met a car I didn't buy or a cruise I didn't take. This, without regard to the state of my bank account. Credit cards were my catnip. I was a charter member of the Diners Club, whose card became the nation's first plastic narcotic. My house in Pacific Palisades, California, was so encumbered by mortgages that it would have taken me forty years to own it.

My business manager, a busty blonde, encouraged my spendthrift ways, especially when she was the beneficiary. What cured me (and fired her) was the skinny brunette whom I later married. Her name is Helen Gurley Brown.

The cure took a while. My former indifferences to foolish spending is unfortunately of epidemic proportions among Americans. Consumer debt is at a record high. I see this debt affliction among many of my friends. They haven't a clue as to where they will find the money to finance their living standard, let alone their retirement.

It's sad to be dumb about money. Spending is addictive and bad for the heart and brain. Learning to handle money intelligently is a difficult but rewarding talent to hone.

Benjamin Franklin had it right. A penny saved is a penny earned.

3. minding my purse

given my spendthrift habits, you might well wonder how I managed to keep a marriage to a thrifty woman going for nearly half a century.

What first attracted me to Helen Gurley Brown, apart from her good looks and her style, was the revelation that she had paid cash for her Mercedes-Benz 190SL. I had never before met a girl who paid cash for so much as a pack of cigarettes, never mind a car. I thought, "Here is a free-spending and solvent creature." Ah, was I mistaken. Solvent, yes, but I later learned that she cried for days after paying out that cash. I discovered—far too late—that I was involved with a saver and a skinflint.

My wife and I are both Depression babies—born and brought up when nearly everyone was broke and more people were out of work than had jobs. Helen came from dirt-poor Arkansas, while I was from Wall Street's favorite playground, Long Island. Even after my family's home was sold to pay taxes following the crash, I would regularly forget that I was no longer rich—and I spent accordingly. This hang-up stayed with me for years.

When Helen and I married, she couldn't understand why a highly paid Hollywood executive had no savings and was, in fact, in debt. (Two divorces were among my extravagances.) She had been deceived by my spending habits. To this day she becomes furious when she recalls the $200 Christmas gift I gave the maître d' at the long-since-closed Romanoff's, a far costlier gift than the string of faux pearls I'd given her.

I continued to bestow pricey presents on captains, waiters and, in one fiery incident, the busboy at Mark's, a private London club, who never forgot the £20 note he pocketed for clearing the table. Our argument about the tip began at the table. Helen and I continued it in the reception hall, where she virtually screamed as she headed out the door, stomping her way back to Claridge's all alone. For my part, I was left to contemplate never being allowed back in Mark's, considering that no major enthusiasm exists in the United Kingdom for screamers of either sex. (Truth be told, I did get back in. The busboy must have put in a good word.)

It gets worse. Sometimes when I have left $30 on a dresser for the maid in a hotel where we've stayed for only one night, Helen does a little reconnaissance after I've walked out into the hall with our luggage. Picking up one of the tens, she'll insist it is *her* money that I am throwing out the window.

Of course, she can change direction in a microsecond when something doesn't cost what she thought it would. For example, Helen's improbable romance with caviar began years ago at New York's posh Le Pavillon restaurant. A captain appeared with a big blue can of beluga caviar and proceeded to ladle out giant portions.

Helen was aghast. She imagined a bill approximating the United States GNP. She was in the act of protesting energetically when the captain explained, "Mr. Brown's secretary gave Mr. Soule (the restaurant's proprietor) a tour of the 20th Century-Fox studio, and Mr. Soule wishes to say thank you." From that moment on, Helen's taste for caviar escalated, augmented by free, mega portions on the *QE2,* where she often lectures.

As for me, I never miss an opportunity to waste money. At a dinner honoring me at the New York's Dutch Treat Club, my friend Gene Shalit observed that the occasion was an anomaly inasmuch as I always pick up the check and never "go Dutch." Okay, maybe I'm a little over the top with dispensing money. Given the choice, I'd take the Concorde to London or Paris, although I'd accumulated a million American Airlines frequent-flier miles.

The upside of having a parsimonious wife is that it has turned me from being an economic illiterate into someone who has learned the value of money. After we opened a savings account, I enjoyed seeing our balance go up each week. And when Helen offered to make out checks to pay our bills, I said goodbye to my business manager, who'd received 5 percent of my income for paying bills. (The fact that she was blonde and foxy hastened her departure.)

Helen's ways have not changed. When the kitchen of our Pacific Palisades home needed redoing, she hired a handy local fireman rather than a costly kitchen specialist. She never discards paper clips. If I place the day's change on our hall table, she appropriates it for bus fare—at the senior rate, of course. Flight attendants, knowing her hoarding habits, give her mini gin and Scotch bottles.

So far as I can remember, Helen has never bought any office supplies for home use. Some of the pencils, erasers and memo pads that we have in our apartment date back to Helen's secretarial years at the Foote, Cone & Belding advertising agency. Our biggest arguments are over whether to take a taxi or bus. The bus wins. She'd take a bus in a blizzard on New Year's Eve.

So there you have it: a penny-pinching wife and a spendthrift husband. The money she saves, I squander. So how do we manage money and marriage? My rules for preventing this issue from erupting into relationship-bursting flare-ups are:

1. If your mate or life partner is on an asset-wasting spree, he (or she) must be stopped. Credit cards must destroyed, charge accounts closed, bank accounts frozen. Terminal profligacy must be treated as an addiction. Intervention must be arranged, with family members and financial advisors in attendance.

2. Big-time compulsive gambling is incurable. A divorce lawyer is the only possible therapist. Act swiftly, before your house is gone.

3. This is for wives: Is your husband secretive about his financial status? A change in his spending may signal munificence toward another woman. Insist on complete disclosure.

4. Are you being dunned by creditors when you have no recollection of spending money or incurring debt? You may be the victim of a spouse's prodigal habits. Again, zero in on your income and outcome.

5. Remember you are liable to the IRS if your mate doesn't pay taxes.

Despite the acrimonious difference between our spending habits, Helen and I pool our funds. Our bank accounts, stock portfolio and real estate are held jointly with either of us able to clean out the other with one signature and no recourse.

Obviously, this arrangement succeeds because of our total trust in each other. How else could Helen put up with my ordering a $150 bottle of Chateau Lafite Rothschild at New York's '21' Club when I was freshly unemployed? Richer or poorer, we are the spend/thrift couple. For us, it works.

4. when experts are stubbornly wrong

i've noticed that those most sure of themselves are often wrong. If experts were infallible, airplanes would never fly, dot.com companies would never sink and calories wouldn't count. In those and endless other instances, experts were on the wrong side.

That is one of the reasons contrarian opinion rules Wall Street. Whenever there is a consensus among well-respected stock analysts, the smart money votes the other way. If everyone agrees stocks are going up, they go down. And vice versa.

In medicine, there is almost always a need for a second opinion even if the first opinion is from an esteemed source.

The largest ship of its time, the *Titanic*, was certified as unsinkable. It wasn't.

The Literary Digest, one of America's leading weekly magazines, predicted that Alf Landon, the Republican candidate, would defeat Franklin D. Roosevelt's bid for a second term as President. It was wrong and its miscalculations put it out of business. (Roosevelt went on to win a 3rd and 4th term.)

The *Chicago Tribune* was so certain that Thomas Dewey would defeat Harry Truman in the 1948 Presidential election that it went to press with the headline: DEWEY WINS! Wrong.

Military intelligence specialists failed to predict the attacks on the World Trade Center and Pentagon. Even National Security Advisor Condolezza Rice said nobody could imagine airliners being used as weapons—nobody but lower-level experts whose warnings went unheeded.

Back in 1941, intelligence experts didn't have a clue that the Japanese would unleash a sneak attack on Pearl Harbor.

Medieval experts believed the world was flat and the Catholic Church burned people alive for suggesting otherwise.

Does this mean experts are *always* wrong? No. It means they are as fallible as non-experts

Broadway superstar Mary Martin listened to a preview of a new musical score by Frederick Loewe with lyrics by Alan Jay Lerner for a show to be called *My Fair Lady*. She later remarked to her husband, "Isn't it sad? The poor boys have lost their talent." The show opened in 1956, broke all Broadway records and is still playing with its songs being sung every night somewhere in the world.

In a small book titled *Rotten Opinions,* it is revealed that noted critics trashed Mozart, hated Shakespeare, and derided Thomas Edison.

A Hollywood talent scout concluded that Fred Astaire couldn't dance.

Remember Ira Gershwin's memorable lyric, "They all laughed at Christopher Columbus when he said the world was round; they all laughed when Edison invented sound . . . They all laughed at Fulton and his steamboat, Hershey and his chocolate bar. Ford and his Lizzie kept the laughers busy, that's how people are."

Don't you be that way.

5. lessons from a life in showbiz

i'm in show business and while what follows may not be immediately understood by civilians, it will give them an inside view of the entertainment world:

An exec who is unwilling to put his job on the line for a project he believes in should lose his job.

One person's vision, right or wrong, is worth more than a consensus of 12. Trust passion.

Relying on others' opinions is a lazy and disastrous practice. Darryl F. Zanuck ordered readers' opinions to be removed from synopses. Barry Diller, while at Paramount, read full material—books, plays or scripts—before deciding to proceed with production.

Satisfying work is never a substitute for living or loving, and yet without it life is barren.

Applause in the dailies is no guarantee of the success of a film but a better indication than no applause.

Where is it written that an over-50 director with many films to his credit is not preferable to an under-30 director with only a festival award in his résumé? Same for writers.

Casting in payment for sex is a bad idea. It's been tried by some of the greats of the business and found to lead to poor performances on the screen and in bed.

Never be mean, chintzy and ugly to your secretary or she'll write a book.

Verbal pitches rarely make it to the screen and are frequently forgotten in the passage.

Nobody but the filmmakers can be trusted to form a valid opinion of a film by seeing a rough cut or reading a script. Especially marketing people. Show them the finished movie only, and even then treat their opinion as suspect.

Enthusiasm is the fuel of show business, especially unwarranted enthusiasm. Without it you can't go to work in the morning.

The larger the number of executives in a production department, the poorer their movie.

Bureaucracy dilutes the creative process—and slows decision-making to a pathetic trickle.

This is from Darryl F. Zanuck: Interesting subject matter of a movie is more important than brilliant execution. I'd rather have a fair script on a provocative subject than a brilliant one about the sex life of an earthworm. I've had both.

Being a waiter, book salesman or dealer in a casino is better preparation for a producing career than four years in film school. The best producers often are rogues and super salesmen.

Women are better judges of scripts than men, and 12-year-olds know more about casting.

The worst preview audiences are your friends and relatives. Don't invite them.

Fame and fortune are temporary and in time will go. Stars and tycoons eventually will be forgotten. The only legacy is your care and love for your fellow man (and woman). Remember columnist Walter Winchell's line, "Be nice to those you meet on the way up—they're the same ones you meet on the way down." He wasn't—and proved the truth of his utterance. His burial was attended by a Rabbi and only one of his three children.

Scripts with camera angles and verbose stage directions are the sign of an amateur.

Booze isn't bad—in moderation. Smoking—even in moderation—is. Water is boring. When health clubs took the place of bars, the quality of movies suffered. So sue me.

Meetings are the bane of the film business, along with voice mail. Between meetings and dailies, it's almost impossible to communicate on a personal level with studios. Nothing is decided except in person. Finding or hearing a live human being is all but impossible.

Never entrust a business manager with discretionary power. Anyone who makes creative decisions can decide about his own investments. It's easier. How you handle your money can be fun.

Not returning phone calls is the sign of a loser. It's always easier to get the CEO or boss of a studio than an underling. That's why they're underlings.

You're only as good as your last picture—depending on how long ago your last picture was.

Those entrusted with green-lighting pictures should become involved with the process at the beginning instead of at the end. This would save scads of money spent by development executives with only the power to say no. In films as well as in television, it is ludicrous for the decision-makers to sanction this waste.

No matter how successful you are as a producer you're always Willy Loman begging for your next gig.

Irving Berlin said, "The trouble with success is that you have to keep being successful." A tragic truism.

Most actresses (and actors) are smarter than most executives. I don't know why that is, but it is.

6. on being a gentleman

anita loos claimed that gentlemen prefer blondes but marry brunettes. Cole Porter said most gentlemen don't like love—they just like to kick it around. And George Bernard Shaw added an androgynous note when he defined a gentleman as "a man, more often a woman, who owes nothing and leaves the world in debt to him."

Getting around as I do in restaurants, theaters, airports, and yes, on buses and subways, I detect that manners are improving as we glide through the first years of the 21st century. Whether it's because of the increased presence of women in the workplace, I believe gentlemanly behavior—practiced by men *and* women—is on the rise.

Times have changed, as Cole Porter *also* said, but standards of gentlemanly behavior have not. Such behavior is as cool and hip today as it ever was. In fact, one of the best examples of it I can recall took place more than three decades ago. Back then, the first mezzanine of New York's Art Deco Radio City Music Hall was reserved for A-list power figures. They were escorted aloft from a walnut-paneled VIP lounge by way of an elevator the size of a phone booth. It was operated by an equally diminutive pageboy. On one occasion, the pageboy's lone passenger put out his hand in greeting and said, "Hello. I'm Dwight D. Eisenhower." Whether a former President or a plain old citizen, a gentleman does not assume he is recognized on sight—as true now as ever.

There are times, however, when he does not wish to be identified. Cary Grant, seated beside a dowager at a Park Avenue dinner party, was asked, "And what is it you do, Mr. Grant?" (That in itself was a social no-no). The mega-movie star, unwilling to inflict the pain of a gaffe on his questioner, replied, "Oh, I'm in the perfume business." It was true, although his role as a board member of Fabergé was not the one for which he was famous.

Cary Grant notwithstanding, gentlemen do not always come clothed in formal dress or, these days, Armani. They often wear blue collars. I have observed more politeness on Hollywood sound stages or construction site than in some boardrooms or fashionable restaurants.

How, then, does one make the cut? Here are my rules: Never be rude, regardless of provocation. This will infuriate the provoker, who gets off on bleats of wounded feelings.

Always acknowledge a gift, be it something in a blue Tiffany box or a single yellow rose from the corner vendor.

Dress within reason (no black tie in the jungle), according to the inner man—your own true self. I dress conservatively even on movie sets, as did Alfred Hitchcock, because *c'est moi.* Don't be intimidated by the reigning dress code.

Speak softly. This was true even on the Concorde, where voices also travel at twice the speed of sound. It is especially true when using a cell phone.

Say "please" and "thank you," words that Andy Rooney believes have nearly dropped out of the language.

Do not talk or eat with your hands. My wife of thirty-nine years delicately fingers salads; less presentable types engaging in this practice may unfortunately resemble Henry VIII.

Avoid a stuffy, patronizing demeanor, although if you have one, you'll probably have to be exorcised to lose it. A gentleman may be daring in conversation but is always respectful of unpopular opinion. He may be fearless about taking a contrarian stand but will never do so in an abrasive way. Above all, he does not put his listeners to sleep.

Treat everyone equally. A gentleman makes no distinction among classes. As Professor Higgins said in defense of his dealings with Eliza Doolittle in *My Fair Lady:* "It's not as though I treat you differently from anyone else. I treat you the same."

Keep your word, especially if you've made a bad bargain.

Return all phone calls the same day (except those from argumentative callers), and reply to all but pest letters. (Show-business types tend to be especially delinquent in this department.)

Be unconcerned about taking credit, yet give it freely even to those who are undeserving but need it.

View the world with wit and laughter: without a robust sense of humor, a fellow is a bust who doesn't know how to score.

Never reveal your net worth to anyone but your accountant and, depending on the state of your marriage, your spouse. Braggarts are boors, especially those who talk about how wealthy they are. Romantic dalliances (they used to be called "conquests" before feminists got us thinking) are also off conversational limits. Always send flowers after a night of passion, and *don't* steal away once you are sated. As La Rochefoucauld said: "A gentleman may love like a lunatic but not like a beast." Don't be beastly.

Never tell truth that hurts unless it only hurts you. John Henry Newman got it right when he wrote, "It is almost a definition of gentleman to say that he is the one who never inflicts pain."

Be more interested in *doing* right than being right.

I'm happy to report that I know many men who observe these rules. Jack Nicholson, his bad-boy image aside, almost always does; so does Paul Newman (unless you ask for his autograph, which he considers foolish); Tom Hanks is as admirable as the characters he usually plays; Morgan Freeman is the very definition of a gentlemen in dress and deportment; and Clint Eastwood will make your day with his manners and modesty. Cary Grant and Gary Cooper were true models in their day. Gentlewomen include Barbara Walters, Diane Sawyer, Sherry Lansing, and, in their time, Audrey Hepburn and Claudette Colbert.

Inasmuch as I value women's opinions on this subject, my secretary and my wife demand to be heard. My secretary, Doris Wood, offers this definition: "A gentleman is able to express himself with a vocabulary larger than four-letter words." And Helen Gurley Brown's unpredictable take: "A gentleman puts up with your use of four-letter words but uses none himself—except in bed." Go figure.

I can't leave this chapter without quoting Samuel Butler's reverie about gentlemen. "If we are asked what is the most essential characteristic that underlies this word, the word itself will guide us to gentleness, absence of browbeating or overbearing manners, absence of fuss, and generally consideration for the other people."

7. doctors—
can they keep you well or make you sick?

a little background. I wanted to become a doctor, inspired by such books as Sinclair Lewis's *Arrowsmith*. To innoculate me, my father secured a pre-college job for me as a laboratory technician at New York's Bellevue hospital. The view was anything but belle—my lab table faced the window of a ward for terminally ill prostitutes, their looks hideously ravaged by venereal disease.

This did not prevent them from beckoning me obscenely with spider-like arms. My duties consisted of dissecting white mice after injecting them with pneumonia virus. I was also required to make visits to the morgue where I witnessed grisly autopsies. Is there any other kind?

Result: I changed my academic major from pre-med to the softer demands of journalism.

I also developed a fear of doctors that persisted to the eighth decade of my life. It prevented me from visiting a doctor for seventeen years—ending only when I was crippled with abdominal pain and my wife threatened to leave me if I didn't submit at once to a physical examination. I did, and thereafter, in a burst of counter-phobia, saw a doctor every three months.

This brings me to the present, when my physician, the eminent Rees Pritchett, indulges what he terms my "David-itis" by faxing my blood and urine reports before my regular check-up visits. My pre-med training serves me well.

All of the above ruminations qualify me to advise you about doctors. In these litigious times, many physicians are not seeking new patients. You must solicit their care gently. Some of them are as out of sorts as harried flight attendants, pressured by fear of lawsuits or patient rage. Treat your doctor as you would have him or her treat you—with compassion. Assure him you are not a nutcase. Confide in him big time. Your account of what ails you is the most reliable guide to your treatment.

Doctors are not infallible. Mistakes are made. The medication he prescribes may not work or may produce unwanted side effects. Stop taking it and tell him it's anathema to you. If a number of mistreatments take place, don't get a second opinion—get a second doctor. Your best doctor, in my opinion, is a teaching professional—that is, a physician on a hospital teaching staff who has a few private patients. Those MD's are usually on salary and their fees for services are far less than those in private practice.

Doctor's can't help you if 1) you smoke surreptitiously (although some of *them* do outside hospital gates); 2) if you're ridiculously overweight; 3) if you downplay your symptoms; 4) if you ignore their instructions.

Don't be put off by your doctor's health or lack thereof. I outlived at an early middle age doctors who were no older than I. Some died of heart attacks. Others of cancer. Hospitals are dangerous places. Some physicians are notoriously careless about their own health habits but still are good doctors. It's a case of don't do as I do but as I say.

Doctors are, of course, the ultimate rulers of our fate. Kings and tyrants, Popes and dictators must at some point submit to their ministrations. No man is a hero to his valet—or a commanding presence to his internist. I regard their wisdom with awe and tremble in anticipation of their findings. And yet, doctors need doctors too and must submit to them, and yes, get sick and even die. I've lost two of them. Which makes me wonder. Why do so many of them eat and smoke too much? They're human—that's why. As for their omniscience, ponder this. Doctors bury their mistakes. Architects grow ivy.

8. regrets, i've had a few. here are some.

dancing like a klutz. Why does the drum in my head not connect with my feet?

Not having children pains me now but pleased me in my carefree earlier years. My son, whom I lost (to drugs). His is a love I never replaced.

Not being able to play a piano. The magic of making those keys dance with the magical sounds of Cole Porter, Irving Berlin, Jerry Herman, George Gershwin, Noel Coward and Hoagy Carmichael.

Not having a mega-hit Broadway musical. My idea of career heaven—better than Oscar, Pulitzer or Nobel. And months after I wrote the previous sentence, I did get my mega-hit Broadway musical in *Dirty Rotten Scoundrels!*

Losing old friends too young to go. The memories never fade.

Caring too much what others think and caring too little for my own convictions.

Not having a country house, a retreat in the woods. My wife, who was a country girl and happily out of it, says if I want a place in the woods with all the attendant chores, I should get a wife.

Not to have continued my journalism career. Biggest wish—to be editor of *The New Yorker, Time* or *Esquire.*

Not having a daughter. My eyes mist at the thought of bringing her up, attending her graduation and reluctantly surrendering her on her wedding day.

Not being a natural athlete, which would have given me grace of movement and confidence in my physical power. I especially miss the ability to box and wrestle so that I could have banished the bullies of my childhood.

Not having a father during my formative years—my natural father, that is. It would have given me courage and strength if he loved and supported me.

Most of all, and previously mentioned, I grieve that I could not have saved my only son, Bruce, from his fate. As Jerry Herman's poignant lyric has it, "Did I give enough? Did I give too much? At the moment that he needed me, did I ever turn away? I'll ask myself my whole life long, what went wrong along the way?"

9. hollywood, under the tinsel

movies have fascinated the world since Edison invented his magic lantern. Hollywood is where the legend lives—its people, its lifestyle, its wildness. Movie stars have long been the world's royalty as kings and queens went into decline.

Movies are the magnets. Example: My wife and I were in Tahiti, on a tour bus in a remote section of that exotic, remote island. Ahead was a throng of half-naked natives. Fearing some accident, or road kill, we moved closer. There, lined up, in front of a shed they patiently stood. A sign on the shed read, "Now playing, TITANIC."

I have worked, played and married in Hollywood for more than 50 years. Studios were my playground, workplace, and sometime havens from belligerent mates. Studios of that era had their own police force, hospitals, restaurants—all behind guarded walls and impenetrable gates through which only the select few could pass—the moguls, the movie stars and their legion of worker bees.

Those were the days when movies were movies. Today, Hollywood is a bank ruled not by wacky tyrants but by marketing gurus, entertainment lawyers and money counters. Hollywood was always about money but the spenders were the creative types and not their minders. When Richard Zanuck and I were running 20th Century-Fox studios, we were approached by a young banker named Denis Stanfill who suggested that he or someone like him be stationed where the money was spent, at the studio, instead of the distant New York headquarters where the money was collected. We accepted this dictum, hired him and were soon fired by him for *our* spending habits. Soon thereafter, the Stanfill doctrine was adopted industry-wide. Why leave those idiots alone with the company checkbook?

In came the hostile hordes of distribution mavens, treasurers, finance v.p.'s, and more presidents and vice presidents in charge of parking lots, catering trucks, development and various other nothings. Gone were the iconoclastic, semi-literate, rogues and roustabouts who made Hollywood great—of whom super mogul Louis B. Mayer once observed, "They may be idiots but they made millions for us." They also made good movies you didn't have to be a 12-year old to appreciate.

Yes, Hollywood has changed. It's no longer run by the

inmates. It's *owned* by them. The lifestyle has changed with it. For example, a top executive made an urgent appointment with his boss; approaching her with foreboding, he—a family man with children—confessed that he was gay.

"Thank God," exclaimed his boss, "I'm so relieved. I thought you wanted to quit." This is a true story.

When I arrived in Hollywood in late 1951, smoking and drinking were still *in*. Every home had a bar—now transformed into a workout room. Decadence was the order of the day—and night. Drugs were only beginning to replace alcohol, but slowly; Hollywood was partyland. Restaurants—Romanoff's, LaRue, Perino's, Chasen's—were elegant and, unlike today, the customers better dressed than the waiters. In Spain, the South of France, London, Paris, Hollywood shed any homeland inhibitions and went wilder. Sex was the narcotic—more of it off screen than on.

The players were bigger than life—Flynn, Chaplin, Gardner, Mitchum, Sinatra, Crawford, Russell, Hughes, Spiegel and so many others. They lived, loved, gambled, smoked, drank with nary a qualm about fitness or health. AIDS did not exist and early Alzheimer's was frequently unnoticed and not much different from ordinary behavior in Hollywood.

Gangsters were movieland's royalty and part of the A-list. After all, when Virginia Zanuck remarked to Bugsy Siegel , "But you kill people!" he repeated what he'd said to construction mogul Del Webb. It was his oft quoted response: "We only kill each other."

Like the poetess Edna St. Vincent Millay, "We burned the candle at both ends, but oh what a lovely light!"

10. sex, love and marriage— the potency myth

start with sex. As editor, and best-selling author Gene Fowler once observed, "One strand of pubic hair can be stronger than the Atlantic cable." Someone else said, "A stiff penis has no conscience." Then there is Bruce Jay Friedman's admonition, "Don't let that little frankfurter ruin your life."

While those aphorisms are male-directed, they apply equally to women. Sex is wonderful but you have to be careful not to have it destroy you. The head on the pillow next to yours on the morning after must belong to a nice person, a "mensch," someone with understanding, compassion, and wit. Otherwise, you're fucked in both the literal and figurative sense.

Sex is the tender trap. It can lead to a lifetime of joy and warm companionship or to a nightmare of misery and regret. You have to be lucky. Here are a few pointers to keep in mind to attract luck:

Look at her (or his) bathroom. If it's a mess—dirty

towels, ring around the tub, strands of toilet paper trailing about—beware of getting involved. The bathroom is an accurate reflection of what your relationship will be like.

Can she make you laugh? Laughter is the glue of love. It helps if you're funny too. Humor gets you through the bumpy times. It also gets you into bed sooner. When you think about it, a hearty laugh is like a sexual climax. You feel good all over. A squeeze is next. Find your favorite fantasy—and hers. Nothing is illegal, immoral or fattening in fantasy world. Barring chains and whips, go for it.

Smartness is another essential quality for good sex, good marriage or simply a good relationship. Pleasurable après sex is as important as cozy après ski. It can be ruined by dumb or boring remarks that make you wish you hadn't got involved. There's an old Latin saying, *post coitum omne animal triste* (after an orgasm, everyone is sad). Don't let that happen to you. A woman or man with a brain makes love-making infinitely more exciting. Go for the smarts—not intellectual but just smart. Like sexiness, you'll know it when you encounter it. To paraphrase an old ad phrase, it's sexy to be smart.

Money is an aphrodisiac. Fuck-you money is very fuckable. Someone with the shorts can be deflating . . . and expensive. She or he needn't be a millionaire, but, once again, as the song says, a little filthy lucre buys a lot of things, including good sex.

Sex is power. The ability to arouse an otherwise impotent, older, rich man can make you millions. Fake that orgasm and *you* can bathe in riches!

Here's a downer you might not expect. Lateness in a woman is a cardinal sin, especially in the menstrual cycle. Being on time in man or woman is a blessing. I've been involved with—well, I've been married to—women who keep me waiting on street corners, in restaurants, even at weddings. No fun. Marilyn Monroe was the ultimate latecomer. Poor darling, for her it was a sickness. A one time head of 20th Century-Fox told me he had a scheme to get her to work on time. My director, George Cukor, and I responded in unison, "If you put her in a bed on the set and pre-lit it, she'd be late."

Grating loud voices in either sex are de-sexifying. I don't want to be with a screamer, whiner or graveler. Foul language isn't acceptable except perhaps in bed. A bit of Hollywood wisdom. Never sleep with anyone who has less money or more trouble than you have.

What about the potency myth. Yes, *myth*. There are infinite ways to make love pleasurable without penetration. A perhaps surprising observation: sex is not necessary for a sexual relationship. What? Why? How come?

Some of the more romantic, even erotic relationships are fired by *denial* or separation. The noted playwright George Bernard Shaw had an intense love affair that was never consummated. Tristan and Isolde of Wagnerian love could never get it together.

Sex can be ignited by the touch of a hand, a kiss, the lighting of a cigarette or an erotic telephone call. In Orson Welles's great film, *Citizen Kane,* a character muses that he had seen a girl on the Staten Island ferry 40 years earlier and not a day passed since that he did not think of her.

One of the greatest love stories, that of Romeo and Juliet, is also not hard-core sex, in fact, no sex. Simply desire. Same-sex love must also be included in the pantheon of eroticism. Love and let love in your fashion. It makes the head go round, if not the world.

Holding hands at midnight or any other time can make the juices flow. And the kiss, ah the kiss, properly administered, can rock you to the tip of your shoes. As for the act itself, penetration is the classic way but other means can be equally and sometimes more exciting. There's oral sex, whose skillful practitioners have toppled CEO's from presumed rock-bound marriages, nearly removed a leader of the free world from office, and turned dictators into jelly beans.

There are, in addition, endless other means of auto or mutual satisfaction. When Sigmund Freud observed that most people practiced masturbation, one of his students indignantly retorted that he had never masturbated. "Well then," commented Dr. Freud, "You missed a good thing."

Sometimes, a waning of our powers is not a bad thing. The famed screenwriter, Nunnally Johnson, on being asked by his daughter if he'd ever renew his friendship with Darryl Zanuck, replied, "Only when he's impotent."

Intimacy, wit, passion, aphrodisiacs. Addenda. I never mentioned youth in this discourse on sex. Sex goes on regardless of age, leading to the final perfect erection, rigor mortis. My partner, Richard Zanuck, and I produced a movie that might have been titled, "Sex and the Older Man." It was called *Cocoon.* In visiting retirement homes in preparation for the movie, we discovered that there was more sexual activity and X-rated appetite raging there than in Hollywood.

11. stress-makers

stress is the enemy of health and happiness. Everybody experiences some. Most stress is caused by an exaggerated feeling of peril. Fear of falling and darkness are the stresses of childhood, followed by fear of failure and rejection during school years.

Grown-up fears are the most malevolent. Although I worked in a hospital lab and morgue in my late teens, I developed the fear of doctors I mentioned earlier. Even now every routine medical examination fills me with dread and pumps up my blood pressure. Stress my doctor calls David-itis.

Anxiety about the health and welfare of loved ones is a stress-maker.

Fear of flying immobilized me for years. I overcame it at first through immoderate consumption of alcohol during flight and finally, through repeated familiarity with changes of engine time and release of landing gears. I even became comfortably accustomed to Concorde's supersonic flight.

I was also being harassed by unpleasant, wacko telephone calls on the ground. Being unreachable in the air lessened my earth-bound tension.

As with good sex and bad sex, there's good stress and bad stress. Good stress is the stress of accomplishment—whether striving for your driver's license or coming first in a 50-yard dash.

Good stress is making love to your wife. Bad stress is making love to somebody else's wife. Success is good stress. Failure is bad stress. Good stress is the adrenaline you produce in an emergency.

Bad stress manifests itself in back pain, shortness of breath, heart palpitation, headache. Reducing it can be managed by a brisk walk or jog, a hot bath, yoga, biofeedback, prayer—whatever works.

There is much controversy about my next suggestion. I like a stiff belt of Scotch whiskey to calm me. Before it was forbidden by law and medicine, a cigarette was a great stress-remover.

So sue me!

12. friendship— why some enemies are more reliable

there are many types of friends. There are childhood friends. They usually fall away. Death or distance removes them from your life. Changed circumstances are a barrier to long friendship. Those who survive become the best of friends—links to earliest days, when parents were alive and youth and life seemed inexhaustible.

Next are the friends made through common experience in the Armed Forces, work, romance. These friendships last as long as the bond is work, combat or romance. They can be intense—especially in trying times, threats of jeopardy, big wins or losses—all are the ties that bind.

Friendship can be a late bloomer. George Washington counseled, "True friendship is a plant of slow growth and must undergo and withstand the shocks of adversity before it is entitled to the appellation (of friendship)."

Friendships unfortunately are as susceptible to divorce as marriages. My wife had what she considered a strong friendship. It was inexplicably and suddenly broken. She discovered the reason was her refusal to contribute money to a political candidate. Political differences can wound friendships, and, as in this case, even terminate them.

Money issues are also a menace. A Catalonian proverb holds, "If you would have enemies, lend money to your friends." Shakespeare concluded that such loans result in the loss of both money and friends.

One of the unexplained areas in the world of friendship is the opposite sex. In some parts of the world, notably Los Angeles, it is considered odd, if not suspicious, to have lunch or a deep friendship with a woman not your wife or business associate. The only conclusion is that the couple must be lovers.

I adore women as friends and while I think of them as potential lovers, I consider the perils and snap back to safe buddydom. A friend from across the gender line can be a delight and a treasure. They can be confidantes, advisors and trusted pals. I share with them secrets I would disclose to nobody else.

I lunch with them often. Dinner is out, my wife decrees—unless out of town or on nights when she (my wife) goes dancing (with somebody else). I keep making girlfriends—when someone neat comes along.

Friendship ripens with age. My friend, commentator Andy Rooney, once said, "The most surprising thing that happened to me is the number of good friends I've made after we were both 70 years old. I didn't know you continued to make friends that late in life."

I'm proud to be one of them.

13. sleep is for sissies

"i can't sleep." is the complaint of millions. I say, so what? Sleep is deducted from your life span. When deep, it is a sampling of death. When troubled and nightmarish, it is a prelude to hell. As for dreams, Shakespeare had it right when he intoned, "Perchance to dream; ay there's the rub; for in that sleep of death what dreams may come . . . Must give us pause."

Dale Carnegie, best-selling author of years gone by, advised, "If you can't sleep, then get up and do something. It's the worry that gets you, not the loss of sleep."

There are, I have found, sleepers and non-sleepers. My wife, Helen Gurley Brown, is a sleeper. During our courting days, she fell asleep at parties to the discomfiture of her hostesses. She also sleeps on takeoff of planes and during nights at the opera.(I forgive her the latter.)

The famed songwriter, Irving Berlin, was a world-class insomniac. Although those who knew him best claimed he was asleep but dreamed he was awake.

My prescription for sleep is 1) avoid coffee or tea at dinner, 2) listen to soft music, and 3) visit your past life by dredging up memories of deceased friends and loved ones, particularly lovers.

Be careful about talking in your sleep lest you call out the name of a former lover. This will arouse your wife or present lover and rob them of sleep and you of more.

Mattresses in good hotels are the best. So is the sound of breaking waves. I have a friend who has recorded surf sounds so he can play them in his city apartment.

Food before bedtime can help.

As previously mentioned, I find it soothing to visit deceased friends and lovers and to revisit my earliest memories. Those beloved and long gone dear ones are alive in my dreams and recalling them lulls me to a happy state of repose. I skip sleeping pills. The hangover is bad but I take amphetamines which make me tenderly drowsy.

Another soporific is a boring acquaintance. Listening to a long recital of a family cruise with children's photos to match is a guaranteed sleep inducer.

Sweet dreams.

14. compulsions and other pleasures

compulsions are things you must do without knowing why. The dictionary defines a compulsion as "an irresistible urge to behave in a certain way, especially against one's conscious wishes."

I'm loaded with them.

When I mail a letter, I have to make certain it goes down the slot of the mailbox. This necessitates putting my fingers down the slot many times, giving rise to a suspicious look if a mailman is present. Lest you think this is a fuddy-duddy manifestation of old age, my mail drop compulsion dates back to my student days when postage for a first class letter was two cents.

Moving right along, I must always check whether a faucet is closed or a stove jet is switched off. I empathize with the hapless servant of Phileas Fogg who left the gas on during their 80-day journey around the world.

I have other compulsions but none to match Hollywood agent "Swifty" Lazar's legendary need for fresh, clean towels to be spread double on men's room floors or some movie star's refusal to shake hands. There is, perhaps, an apocryphal story about press lord Rupert Murdoch and Lazar finding themselves in the same men's room. Neither wished to touch the door leading out and so they waited for someone to enter before antiseptically forging out, the door knob untouched.

Another compulsion I suffer (or enjoy) is the need to push a door 13 times. I have always considered 13 a lucky number but how I came to that conclusion God only knows. The least known compulsion (unknown even to my wife) is the need to pray on my knees and give thanks after a successful medical check-up or to pray for help when fearing danger to a loved one, however unlikely.

I am not religious but I figure thanking God or asking for his help, like chicken soup, can't hurt. There are other compulsions in my inventory such as being unable to read reviews of my new film or play when newspapers reach my door. Add to that the necessity for my physician to fax my blood chemistry report prior to a physical examination, and you have a basketful of compulsions—including some I'm too frightened to report—a compulsion in itself.

As for addiction, ah delicious, lovely addiction. There's my addiction to alcohol—mercifully in moderate quantities. My addiction to Cuban cigars wore itself out—too difficult to obtain (illegal in the United States) and impossible to find a friendly smoking area—the back of the police station is out. Consequently, my addiction is confined to certain restaurants in Europe, Asia and Africa.

A now faded addiction was the Concorde, that needle-shaped missile of luxury for travelers who care deeply about speed and lightly about money. Alas, it is gone with the wind it surpassed. Other addictions include beluga caviar, Tattinger blanc de blanc champagne, skinny girls, pickles, pina coladas, snow, sunsets, chocolate soufflé, and, most of all, my beloved wife who is both a compulsion and an addiction.

She has been definitely beneficial to my health (if habit-forming; we've been together 45 years). My advice to you is to cultivate your compulsions and addictions. They add color and tone to your life. Other common compulsions relate to chocolate, food, tobacco and booze.

Banish nicotine, drugs, gambling and larceny—if you would live long and well.

15. the travel bug— its bite can kill

call me a snob but I agree with producer David O. Selznick who declared, "There are two classes—first class and no class." I have traveled the world broke and flush but always in first class. At that, it is an endangered species. Apart from the late Concorde, the only truly first class service aloft are Cathay Pacific, Singapore Airlines, Malaysia Airlines, Japan Air Lines, ANA, Qantas, Air New Zealand, South African, British Airways and Air France.

In earlier days of flying, the Pan Am Clipper ship oozed style. Passengers dressed up to board a plane. TWA, long gone, served caviar and an elegant supper to its sleeper customers—and there were real beds on the Boeing Constellations. Pan Am 747's, the first to fly non-stop from New York to Tokyo, served dinner on upper deck at tables covered with linen tablecloths.

The short-lived MGM Grand decked up its old DC8s to retro luxury levels with compartments for movie stars and a stand-up bar. Never were so few served by so many. Alas, even billionaire Kirk Kerkorian, who owned MGM Grand, had to bring them to earth before his money ran aground.

If you must fly economy class, take this advice from *Consumer Reports:* "Getting stuck in a lousy seat on a long flight is no picnic. Squeezed between passengers like the filling in an Oreo, prevented from reading or eating by the person whose seat back lies in your lap and bathed in fumes from the lavatory . . . here's the advice, select your seat when you buy your ticket. Ask not to be placed near the lavatory or galley. Fly midday or midweek, when business is slow and you have your choice of seats—maybe an empty next seat."

You can count on this. When a voice from the cockpit announces a slight technical problem, the problem escalates to a five-hour delay or even cancellation of the flight. There are other ways to travel than by plane. Ships still cross the seas and offer civilized transport. Look for discounted fares.

The Internet is a rewarding place for bargains on cruises and flights. Last-minute bookings are the cheapest. On ships, beware of cabins near the engine room— you'll get the shakes. Always consult your doctor before embarking. Some tropical destinations require immunization shots, especially to protect against malaria, a nasty affliction. Use credit cards in foreign countries—they afford better exchange rates than your hotel or airport.

NEVER misplace your passport. It is your guardian angel. And don't fight with crew members, especially on airplanes. You can be jailed in a New York minute. Bring soap to most foreign destinations. Their soaps tend to be stingy.

In English-speaking cities, with the exception of Los Angeles, public transportation is the way to go—buses or subways. My wife and I discovered this even in non-English speaking cities—Paris and Moscow, for example. Maps can be read in any language.

As for taxis, beware of non-certified cabs or over-solicitous drivers. They can bilk you or endanger your life. Rude or unlikable drivers are more reliable and cheaper. In some cities—Paris notably—cabs are not hailed in the street. You must line up at cab stands and *never* go in front of a line.

Since most travel is an ordeal nowadays, travel sparingly. Even on luxury ships such as the *QE2* or the newer *Queen Mary*, a computer failure will render the embarkation process helpless. It happened to us. Airports are a jungle—from Beijing to JFK.

Go if you must but be patient.

Bon voyage!

16. how to die slowly

every living thing must die. That's the scary reality. Our cells start dying almost from birth. The trick is to halt their demise, and so, put off the end to life. It's not a cure. As the poet Thomas Gray wrote in his elegy in a country church yard, "All that beauty, all that wealth e'er ever gave; Await alike the inevitable hour, The paths of glory lead but to the grave." But *slowly,* if you try.

Sleep is essential, that precursor to death—except for dreams, as Shakespeare warned. Cells rebuild while the body sleeps. I'm not certain that is medically true but it ought to be. As I said before, I have a wife who is a champion sleeper. . She shows little signs of aging. Drinking alcoholic beverages is recommended—although assuredly not by my wife, who is something of a teetotaler. My authority for recommending booze, except for those genetically or biologically allergic to alcohol, is strictly medical.

The *New England Journal of Medicine,* no barroom chronicle, reports on a study of 38,000 men over 13 years that drinking any kind of alcoholic beverage fortifies the heart and defeats Alzheimer's. Two drinks a day are suggested. No mention is made of women but one must assume alcohol is an equal-opportunity benefactor. To think otherwise is to be the grossest kind of male chauvinistic pig. So belt a few and keep those demons at bay.

I don't know what to tell you about worriers. They do seem to live a long time but who calls that living? My wife is a world-class worrier, well into her 80s.

Most premature death is preventable. This includes reckless driving, especially while drinking. Walking can be dangerous on city streets. Look both ways and don't move against the light—especially at corner intersections.

Smoking is a major life-shortener. Long before the campaign against smoking swept the world, cigarettes were jokingly called "coffin nails."

Excess exercise can kill older fitness aficionados— singles at tennis especially.

Avoid helicopters.

Stay out of small aircraft.

Avoid love affairs with other men's wives.

Don't cheat on your own mate. Crimes of passion cut many lives short.

If you need money desperately, stay away from loan sharks—it's your money or your life.

Illegal drugs will cut you down in your prime—and rob you of your prime.

Guns belong in the army, not in your home. Their possession can be a license to kill or be killed.

Most important perhaps is work, especially in your late years. Retirement has killed more people than traffic accidents. All research indicates that continuing to work and use your mind *actively* lengthens life, forestalls dementia and Alzheimer's, and makes living a joy.

If you are laid off or involuntarily retired, start your own business even if it's a hot dog stand, work crossword puzzles, read newspapers and books.

You'll remain in good health if you stay out of retirement homes and retirement.

17. stop being poor little me

if there is one unattractive trait, and there is, it's self-pity. Feeling sorry for one's self doesn't solve any of life's problems. It exacerbates them.

Take "nobody likes me." Have you considered *why?* Are you so opinionated that you don't consider other views? (Keep *extreme* opinions to yourself. They won't make you popular).

What about simple courtesy as opposed to rudeness? Do you greet people with warmth and friendliness or do you ignore them? When meeting someone, are you looking over his shoulder to see if someone more important or attractive is on the scene?

Self-pity feeds on low self-esteem. If you have a decent regard for yourself, chances are the world will share your opinion. And how do you get that decent regard? You get it by doing your job honestly, helping others and not pretending to be anyone but you.

Not taking yourself too seriously is a starting point. Being imperious or phony is a put down.

It's true that feeling poor little me results from being battered about life's inevitable misfortunes. It's how you take those blows that determines your sense of self-worth and in fact your ability to overcome ill fortune.

Action is the key. Playwright Tennessee Williams counseled, "Make voyages. Attempt them. That's all there is." And movie star Steve McQueen observed, "The world is as good as you are. You've got to learn to like yourself first."

One of the causes of the "poor little me" syndrome is the failure to act or follow through on simple tasks—replying to a phone call, delaying an appointment, failing to respond to a job call. There are always excuses.

Another symptom of the "poor little me" is never giving up on past disappointments and grievances. Like the fellow who constantly relives in his mind that day his boss demoted or fired him. They can't give up the hatred they constantly churn for betrayals and wrongs.

My advice. Get over it.

Listen instead to Ralph Waldo Emerson, "Finish each day and be done with it. You have done what you could. Some blunders and absurdities no doubt crept in; forget them as soon as you can. Tomorrow is a new day; begin it well and serenely and with too high a spirit to be encumbered by your old nonsense."

For everyone suffering the "poor little me" syndrome, some tough love is in order. You must be prepared to face criticism from those who love you and wish you well.

"Poor little me" is a recipe for failure and ignominy. Bathe in self pity and you'll drown in it. Instead, admit your weakness and rise again.

I pity those with self-pity and applaud those who rise above it.

That font of all wisdom, William Shakespeare, had it right when he declaimed, "The fault, dear Brutus, is not in our stars, But in ourselves, that we are underlings."

Take responsibility for bad things happening and then change them.

18. is anyone happy?

songwriter irving caesar wrote the lyrics to two songs about happiness: *I Want to Be Happy* and *Sometimes I'm Happy.*

The reality is that is nobody's happy all the time. Happiness comes in waves—like the tide, it goes in and out. Your first love affair, graduation day, a good medical report, a promotion, the first look at your first born—all these are happiness-making.

Downers are: the death of a child or mate, failure of a long-nurtured enterprise, being fired from a job or ending a romance. Other depressive events include the faltering power of an aging body, boredom, sickness and broke-ness, the inability to reach goals, life without love and its attendant loneliness. These are but a few of my least favorite things.

"Happiness is a thing called Joe," goes an E. Yip Harburg song lyric with music by Harold Arlen. There's truth in that lyric. Happiness is best when shared. Irving

Caesar wrote, "I want to be happy but I can't be happy till I make you happy too." Bingo. Another truism from a song-writer. And there was that perceptive song from the Broadway musical *Top Banana,* giving advice that you *Make Someone Happy.*

Find someone to love who loves you back and you've achieved the goal of a serene and blessed life.

Another ingredient of a happy life is a happy work life. Too many people loathe their jobs, spend their days watching the clock and long for the day when they need no longer work. If you want to achieve a solvent retirement, excel in work you love. It pays best because it brings out your best.

For some a happy work life is a destination in itself. Successful people who are highly paid are often heard to say, "I'd do this for nothing." So happiness is not only a thing called Joe but often a thing called job.

If you want to poison the well of happiness, try envy. Envy is a real killer of joy. Someone else has a great success; you're in mourning. Ambrose Bierce, a famed writer of the last century, described happiness in his *Devil's Dictionary* as "That feeling of exhilaration upon learning of the misfortune of a friend."

Hollywood's own version is, "It's not enough that your friend not succeed—he must fail." The German word *schadenfreude* means joy at the decent of a colleague.

Don't revel in the above, as difficult as that may be. Somebody else's misfortune ought not to bring you joy. Take heart at the great words of Russia's great writer, Alexander Solzhenitsyn: "If your back isn't broken, if your feet can walk, if both arms can bend, if both eyes can see, and if both ears can hear, then whom should you envy? Our envy of others devours us most of all. Rub your eyes and purify your heart and prize above all else in the world those who love you and wish you well."

Book publisher Lyle Stuart has written, "There are no happy endings." There is no permanent happiness—good times and bad times ebb and flow. Health issues, money problems, the perfidy of others all impact on your well being. The antidote is your ability to accept change, which is inevitable, and knowing how to rise above anger, envy and despair. As the ancients said, this too shall pass. And it will. It will.

19. what's it all about, alfie?—or the meaning of it all.

after hearing on the 6 o'clock news about the latest rash of violence or glancing at the bad news in the morning's headlines of the newest of nature's catastrophes, you wonder if there is any meaning to our lives.

If, you may dare to ask, if there is a God, why does he or she permit genocide, holocaust, wars and other disasters to ravage mankind? Good people die. Bad people live. Carnage is rampant. Justice is blind.

Obviously, I can't offer you a rational explanation for all this. Instead of fretting, take yourself to the planetarium at New York's American Museum of Natural History. There, seated in a chair among the stars and endless galaxies festooned on the skies replicated above, you realize how inconsequential the earth, its beings and concerns are in the vastness of space and all its mysteries. Life and its treasures and badness may melt in a cosmic flash in the not too distant future—as have other minor stars.

Apply that realization to your own life and realize that you and indeed the earth itself are not the center of the universe. There are questions that will never be answered and mysteries that will never unfold. That's why religion was born—to offer reason and solace for our existence. Religion, as important as it is to the world's masses, is a kind of conceit of mankind. It has even flourished in an age of awesome contradictory scientific discovery. It's possible that whatever Creator exists, wanted it that way.

There is meaning on a smaller scale. The architecture of the human body, for example. The brain itself is a miracle of meaning, each tendril and compartment governing precise functions. Then there is nature—buds that turn into flowers, and animal, insect and bird life with variations more numerous than Mr. Heinz could imagine.

Dwell on these and other manifestations of life and perhaps you will find meaning. Put it all under a microscope and you will find another universe of cells and microbes illustrating the perfect and perhaps divine order of things.

Above and beyond all this, there is the man-made internet, cyberspace and the infinite pantheon of knowledge represented in your local library.

Finally, there is love, the tender regard of one human

for another; the birth of children; despite the inexplicable tribalism that generates mistrust and hatred of men toward each other.

When this planet is but a burnt cinder, long after man's feeble reign has ended, there still will be order in the universe somewhere and meaning nobody can fathom. That is the un-meaning of it all.

20. memories, ah memories

your earliest memory? Think. It will come. Mine is of me as a child of three in a New York subway car filled with people wearing white masks. The year must have been 1919 and the masks were worn for protection against an influenza epidemic that killed more people than the World War which had just ended.

Why is it that I remember something 75-years-ago when I can't remember what I had for breakfast? It's because the landmarks of the mind are never obliterated, even, according to near-death experiences, as we sink into that oblivion.

For me there are other memories—the recollection of an incredibly petite and lovely girl I saw at a family gathering 65 years ago.

My own memory of a ship haunts me to this day. On the Hudson River, a side-wheeler that plied between New York and Albany ages ago, a two-year-old wandered from his stateroom and his parents. I was that two-year-old and residual panic grips me today when I can't find my wife.

Other memories: Hurrying home to my first wife with a $200 Christmas bonus clutched in my hands. It gave me a greater charge than the eight-figure check I received as first profits from my film, *Jaws*.

Receiving a cable from my first wife announcing her marriage, relieving me of alimony payments.

My marriage to my last wife, Helen Gurley Brown, at the Beverly Hills, California, City Hall.

Receiving the Irving Thalberg Award with Richard Zanuck, the Motion Picture Academy's most prestigious award. An unforgettable evening.

The day of my honorable discharge from the United Stated Army after the end of World War II. I gave my uniform to the doorman of my Manhattan apartment building.

Meeting my father for the first time in my memory. He abandoned me at age three. Now he took me to lunch at the old Murray Hill Hotel in New York and announced that he would finance my education at Stanford University. A few years later, I met my step-brother and step-sister for the first time.

Dining on lobsters at the small restaurant on the Isle

St. Honorat off Cannes in the Mediterranean with several beloved friends, most of whom are now gone.

Sunsets in Bali that are equaled by the view from our New York penthouse on Central Park West—magic hour, as we called it in the movies.

The songs of Sinatra, Crosby, Jolson—and the music from the big bands of Artie Shaw, Ted Fiorito, Eddy Duchin, Hal Kemp and Paul Whiteman—the Dorsey's too.

Dancing on the rooftop of Manhattan's St. Moritz Hotel with my first wife to the music of *You Go to My Head*. She did.

My mother's shining face on Christmas Eve as she tucked me in with the message that Santa Claus was on his way.

Her countenance in death—peaceful and smiling.

The birth of my first and only son, Bruce, nine pounds of beautiful baby born in Lying Inn Hospital—inconceivable that he would succumb to drugs decades later. My love for him never dies.

21. everybody needs a shit detector (how you can tell)

excessive use of the pronoun "I" is a good indication of an excess of human waste.

Anyone who boasts about his or her financial success is detectable. Those who can't say anything in less than a few thousand words are candidates.

References to "those people" as a term of disparagement of any individuals of a different race or political party elicits that certain odor.

Stating my God is better than your God is a certain indicator of digestive malfunction.

Abuse of waiters, cab drivers, flight attendants and others large and small is a sure sign of mal-odor.

Snobbishness toward those perceived to be of a lower station or inferior ancestry requires use of a gas mask because of the pervasive stench.

Impugning one's patriotism is indicative of a narrow-minded and bigoted disposition which, yes, stinks.

Any single-minded obsession—religious, medical, health or economic gimmick—smells to high heaven.

Phoniness in any category—dress, accent, affectation of class—has that water closet fragrance.

Summing it up, the shit detector will come up empty if, in Shakespeare's words, "To thine own self be true; And it must follow, as the night the day, Thou canst not then be false to any man."

22. avoiding the crazies

unfortunately, too many people are nutty. I mean seriously off kilter, loony, deluded and sometimes dangerous. There are several varieties of these crazies.

I will identify a few so that you can get out of their way.

There is the woe-is-me, I-can't-get-a-break variety of nudge. They are essentially harmless unless you try to rescue these wounded birds. Their plea for sympathy may lead you to lend them money, attempt to put their lives in order, or worse, become entangled romantically.

There is a distinction between the legitimately downtrodden and those who make a career of their distress. Look for telltale alcoholism or drugs as the root cause. Emotional problems are another. You can't solve these— so by all means, help those who are innocently in trouble, but dodge the nut cases who have done themselves in.

Avoid the time-wasters. Not a terrible lot but annoying. They are chronically late for appointments, unable to complete assignments on time or ever, long-winded in their explanations of their failings. In short, they are bores. As colleagues or friends they are to be avoided or shaken loose.

Beware the deluded. They may be health nuts, religious nuts or political nuts. They are totally committed to a single creed which is either the repository of all evil or the key to paradise. Run, don't walk, from these loonies.

Next come the near-relatives of the previous group—the addicted. These people are not merely deluded—they're hooked. Whether on alcohol, cocaine, crack or tobacco, they can drag down anyone who tries to help. Lives are ruined. There's no escape from their web of abuse and ingratitude. Promises are made to be broken. Resolutions are not honored. They may go into rehab or AA and, yes, it may work. Better not get involved with them, however, until or unless they're clean for a year or longer.

Another nut is the unfettered optimist. They find good in everyone and everything and needn't have to look for a silver lining—it's all around them. I had a secretary like that. Her name was Golda—it should have been Silver. She assured me that my career was on a sharply upward track when, in fact, I was on the brink of being fired. I believed her. As a result of her wacky assurance,

I no longer appreciate cockeyed optimists. I need the gravitas of realism if not pessimism. That's why I'm happily married to a girl for whom the glass is not only half empty—it's leaking badly. There's comfort in her rock-bottom assessment of life. I'm rarely disappointed, and I can handle the happy options.

There are other nut cases to be shunned but I've covered my main ones.

Neurotics are okay but disturbed types can drag you into an abyss populated by inconsolable and wretched misfits who will trap you in their web of misery.

23. diet or die

it isn't true that in every fat man there's a thin man trying to get out. In every fat man there's a fat man trying to get fatter. Why can't some men or women ever lose weight? It's for the same reason some people can't quit cigarettes or cocaine. They're addicted.

It may be an emotional disconnect or genetic flaw that hooks them but the hunger is there and can lead to premature death. It can be overcome but not exclusively by diet. Billions of dollars have been made by diet-meisters promoting low carb, high carb, grapefruit, sugar-free, all protein and other alleged panaceas.

I've tried them all—starting with the drinking man's diet (I liked that), Atkins, South Beach, Weight Watchers and the others. Know what? I lost weight—for a time. Then up I went—to more pounds than I had when I started. I won't brand these diet schemes as fraudulent or phony. They seem to work for some people. However, there is a simpler and less expensive way to carve off dangerous pounds.

The David Brown secret solution is to eat everything but to eat *less*.

> Rule #1 is to get a good bathroom scale and weigh yourself *every day.*
>
> Rule #2 is to *compensate.* If you pig out at lunch, cut way back at dinner. Make up for your gluttony by starving yourself later. It works.
>
> Rule #3 is to skip the bread while you're waiting to be served and when you do eat it, skip the butter as the French do. If it's good bread it will be just as tasty butter-free.
>
> Rule # 4 is to pass up the canapés and drink straight booze—Scotch, bourbon, gin or vodka will do. Fewer calories. Wine is also okay if you skip the booze.
>
> Rule #5 Avoid desserts—except for fresh fruit.

Do count calories; your bookstore has any number of calorie-counting books. And calories do count—so count them. Forget all the seductive diets that tell you that you can eat all you want. Just eat less of everything and anything. That's an order!

24. love for sale

there's no such an animal as free love. It's for sale, but not on sale. The difference between a high-priced hooker and a rich man's wife may well be the asking price. High-maintenance men and women are luxury items.

Is there anything wrong with putting a price on love and sex? Sex becomes love when the price goes up. Love is long-term—sex is not, even within love. I find nothing shocking about this. Everything worthwhile has a price—cars, houses and meals.

So why not love?

When courts dissolve marriages or relationships, money is exchanged. There is a dollar estimate of the worth of the union—which must be paid to terminate it. The popular song, *I Can't Give You Anything But Love,* doesn't quite make it in the divorce courts.

In all romantic relationships, the swains come with a package. A youngster losing his lady is characterized in the musical show *Coco* as being "like losing a watch in Switzerland."

If he is old and wealthy, that's his package. Hers is her youth and beauty. A rich woman can be an aphrodisiac to a younger man. Power is a form of Viagra. It stimulates the sex glands of the powerless. Power, wealth, beauty, and youth all stimulate the penis. Poverty deflates it.

Marrying wealth can be a burden, however, and the hardest kind of work for a young, impecunious, virile young man. If she ceases to attract him physically, he may lose her and his sinecure. As for older men and much younger women, the price is high. He wants to lie down for an afternoon nap when she wants to go skiing.

And that's not all.

I'll make a confession. Young love is often free. Starving together in a garret is a romantic and not very practical notion. It works for a while. As the prospect of parenthood comes around, the prospective papa needs to consider gathering some cash. If he doesn't think of it, the prospective mama does—and so the financial factor arises. Love flies out the window if there is no bread on the table, and therefore, even young love ceases to be free.

And then there is the love of children. That is never free. George Plimpton, the famed writer, and I once attended a reunion of Yale alumni who had just passed the age of 50. Plimpton observed to these half-century graduates, "One good thing about having a little money is that it keeps you in touch with your children." Does it ever!

"Young love, old love, everything but true love" goes the lyric of Cole Porter's *Love for Sale*. True love does exist in the adoration of small, underprivileged children, large dogs, and occasionally grandparents.

Love is a powerful drug, and while it makes the world go around, it makes some of us crazy.

Beware. True or profane love can be hazardous to your health. All who enter its embrace do so at their own peril. The sentiment "be happy, my love" is often a mockery.

25. my love affair with women (yes, women)

i think i've never met a woman I didn't like—or even love. They make great friends and are even more loyal than dogs. You can pet them and they don't bite.

Sometimes, they bark but it is a friendly sound, more like a yelp. When in heat, they will crash through a plate glass window if the right man is in sight. As confidantes, I have found them trustworthy. They won't rat on a man the way men rat on women, spilling dangerous secrets. Why can't a man be more like a woman—compassionate, kind, gentle and sweet. Women don't make war, although they can kill.

All in all, they're an admirable sort.

Women as friends are preferable to men in my view. They're usually more decorative. For married me, they supply needed variety. Based on short acquaintances, they are charmingly unpredictable. You're not in a conversation rut with a new girl or man. There's a whole new life to talk about—hers and then yours. Your domesticity may be at risk because of the delight of getting to know a new friend.

If you're single, you may stop reading. For you, other gender relationships are open sessions with no limits. You can pursue at will. For those who, like me, are married, there are rules to be followed or big trouble will ensue.

Rule one is that a girl friend is not to be considered a date. She's a friend. Do not touch although you may kiss—but not a lingering one. Just a short smack on the lips. Does it go beyond that? In the mind, possibly. I think every man or woman has that fantasy on first meeting someone, whether married or not. What kind of lover—or mate—would she be? You can't be sued for your secret lusts. Keep them secret, though.

Progressing to a romantic relationship is a different ball game. It requires willingness on the other person's part. It also requires courage. Sneaking around for a rendezvous and the necessary lying are unattractive pursuits. When she becomes more than a friend, everyone around you knows it. One telltale sign: she begins eating out of your plate. Romance can mean the death of friendship. Avoid it.

What you can have in your boy-meets-girl friendship is something closer than sex. It is an intimacy born of two free spirits who want only each other's company. I know of a famous TV personality who carried on a friendship with a non-celebrity woman for decades because it was with her that he could truly relax and confide his anxieties and hang-ups (yes, celebrities have those). There may have been a little hanky panky involved, but it was non-threatening to his marriage and career. In my case, I confided to a woman friend that I had lost my job before I told my wife.

Female friends are not jealous of wives but are extremely jealous of other female friends. Therefore, if you want to keep their trust, practice monogamy and don't fool around with other girls (or men). It's okay to go on loving your wife.

The Hungarian playwright Ferenc Molnar is said to have remarked after the death of his wife, "Now I am free to marry my mistress but then where will I spend my evenings?"

It is wise not to talk up friendships with other men or women to your mate. She or he will be naturally jealous and perhaps anxious. Don't lie but don't go into detail about these relationships.

Remember. Your out-of-wedlock friendship is precious. She or he may be your best friend, and as such, even strengthen your marriage. Don't ask me how. That would be revealing a secret.

26. the care and feeding of a famous wife (or how not to feel like a speck)

most men's wives are known only to their family and friends. I'm not married to most men's wives. My wife's name is Helen Gurley Brown and, to her and my astonishment, she is known to Pakistanis, Croatians, Russians, Chinese, Indonesians. It would not surprise me if the Eskimos knew of her too.

The reason for this celebrity has to do with her international, ground-shaking best seller, *Sex and the Single Girl,* and 56 editions of *Cosmopolitan* around the world of which she is the founding editor and editor-in-chief.

At 83, she is still greeted with "You've changed my life" in theaters, on street corners, airplanes, airports and wherever else women and not a few men gather. All this began back in 1962 and has been fed by appearances on television, saucy comments in the press and another six books.

Now, you may ask, where does that leave me, a husband born and brought up on a distinctly un-feminist era when men were supposed to be men and women were expected to walk two steps behind them?

As a boy I knew of only one other lad whose mother *worked* and he concealed that fact. It was a different world then and my wife, among others, had everything to do with changing it. Now when paparazzi turn their cameras away from me to get a one-shot of her, do I cringe? Do I fume? No siree. I smile, I gloat. How come?

It took me two failed marriages before I could no longer consider a wife's starry career an ego-bashing threat. It's not that I'm what my wife would call "a nothing burger." I'm a widely-known producer of films and plays and author of modestly successful books. People do come up to me and say I've changed their life through my seminal *Brown's Guide to Growing Gray,* a reassuring handbook for my fellow octogenarians.

Still, I'm not a brand like my wife and Page Six of the New York Post rarely carries my name.

The reason I don't feel diminished by my famous wife has much to do with her. She's home before I am. She cooks my meals—doesn't like other people around. She takes more pleasure in my achievements than in her own. She's known among hard-core feminists as the Uncle Tom of the women's movement.

How did I get so lucky? Lucky, that's how. Marry in

lust and find yourself wed to a sterling person. Pure luck. That's what it is.

Living with a hugely successful wife is not without perils. There are bad times, stress times when the living is far from easy. Marriages have foundered on the disparity between a prospering wife and a less-than-successful husband.

When a woman makes more money than her husband, it doesn't help to remind her that she married "for better or for worse." Too often, lawyer letters follow. Other than seeking alimony, what's a man to do? I got off my butt and took a job for less than what I formerly earned. That earned respect from my spouse and my temporarily beached career took off.

I was lucky to have a spouse who believed in my ability when the world doubted it. As for living up to the expectations of an acknowledged maven of sexual and romantic perfection, I never felt intimidated. We loved each other and never ranked our ardor on the Richter scale. What I did discover—and this may be true of other celebrity wives (and husbands)—is that they are not at all like the public perceives them to be.

When my wife's book, *Sex and the Single Girl,* was published, letters from her mother and my father told us we were a disgrace in their eyes. "Can't you have the publication withdrawn?" Helen's mother implored. Helen's newly scarlet reputation quickly crossed the Atlantic. J. Paul Getty, then the richest man in the world and an authority on sex (he wrote a column for *Playboy*), invited her to an intimate dinner at his vast London estate. Dinner was quietly downgraded to tea when she mentioned she was bringing her husband.

The truth about Mrs. Brown's libertarian views on sex is that they apply to everyone but me. She doesn't tolerate even the slightest suggestion of hanky panky on my part. Once, she accosted me in a restaurant to inquire indignantly about the identity of my good-looking lady companion. Robert Redford's agent and it was business, I replied. That barely shut her up.

As previously mentioned, her rules about my seeing other women are strict. Lunch is okay but dinner is out, with the exception of her oldest and most trusted friend. Dinner or lunch out of town is definitely not okay. So much for the champion of sexual freedom. She sees nothing strange about this contradiction. Our house is not liberated territory. There's another contradiction. She has a male friend who takes her to lunch in a block-long limousine. Therein lies a tale.

My wife was aboard the ultra-posh Concorde of late lamented memory. She was observed from across the aisle working on a manuscript with paper and pencil. Presto. Shortly after her arrival in New York, there arrived at her office an upscale computer with a note from her Concorde fellow passenger. "I thought you could use this. Let's have lunch." They did—often thereafter. It's not romantic, Helen insists.

Oddly, I'm never jealous of my celebrity wife. I've never felt less of a man because she was more of a woman. That was not true of my earlier marriages. As a younger man, I felt threatened by the very concept of a *working* wife.

My second wife actually left me for one of her public relations clients. As a result, I was in fragile shape when I met Helen Gurley. She was what used to be known as a *career* woman. I worried that her work would undermine our relationship. Happily, it never did.

Before Helen and I married, I sought a submissive, lower profile type. Asian girls seemed a logical choice—until I discovered they were as submissive as Ghengis Khan. French girls were compliant depending on your net worth. German women craved and then administered discipline. I ran the gamut. The dream of attracting a submissive, loving woman vanished like a summer rose.

How, then, was it possible that I married a devoutly independent woman, an icon of the feminist movement, only to discover that she was as submissive as a Geisha, as supportive of her husband as Nancy Reagan and as non-competitive as Mother Teresa?

Again, just lucky I guess.

What I learned about being married to a world-class celebrity is that all celebrities have personas that might surprise their admirers. When Walter Cronkite was called "the most trusted man in America," he was said to have remarked, "If they knew what I really think, I wonder if they would trust me as much."

As a broadcast journalist, he could not reveal how strongly he was at odds with his conservative peers although President Lyndon Johnson told his staff that when Cronkite bashed the war in Vietnam, he, Johnson, knew he'd lost the support of middle America.

My Arkansas born-and-bred wife *is* middle America and never took fame and fortune too seriously, which makes her an authentic, well-loved celebrity.

As for making a difference in people's lives, she sure made a difference in mine.

End of love letter.

27. the end, or maybe the beginning

life is long not short, if you play it right. It helps, of course, to have chosen the right ancestors to give a genetic boost to your life expectancy. If you live long enough, you will have lived many lives with different careers, sometimes different mates and often sharply different circumstances.

In the beginning, everything is possible. Time moves slowly, almost excruciatingly so. One's gait is swift and the mind is a sponge of receptivity. Testosterone rages and the appropriate bodily functions respond with alacrity. It seems as though life will never end—or begin.

Then, in the flower of young manhood or womanhood, it all starts—romance, a first job, fun and games of the strenuous kind. The world is truly your oyster— in your twenties and thirties. The first faint intimidations of mortality arrive in the forties—the big 4–0.

You're still in your prime but not in your prime. Tennis is still your game. Perhaps your drive is not as powerful and your return a trifle slower but you hold your own.

Now come the fifties, the half-century mark. Face it. More than half your life is over. If you're still fit, you may still be playing singles but doubles lie not far ahead. So do prostate concerns, a need for Viagra and a decided bulge in the stomach. More immediate fears. Are you washed up in your career? Flight attendants used to be assigned to desk jobs when they reached age 32. At 50-plus, you are no longer considered young in the job market and possibly even unemployable. Try that on for anxiety.

The sixties are the gateway to old age. Some friends have died. Physical problems crop up. Youthful aspirations too often are unfulfilled. You're where you're going to get and you wanted to get farther. If you don't come to terms with that, emotional problems may dog you.

Old age is not for sissies.

At age 70, as has been memorably written, if you wake up without pains, you're dead. If not dead, you're one of the old ones. Someone gets up to give you a seat on the bus. Other shockers. You can't walk as quickly and you may need a cane.

If you make it into your eighties, you're dealt a different set of problems. Eyes grow dim and foggy. Cataract removal is suggested. Walking now becomes a real drag punctuated by shortness of breath. Your best friend is or should be your doctor and what he tells you is not always reassuring. If you're lucky, your mate is still with you. If not, younger women, like the back of the police station, are out. You don't want someone who doesn't remember Ronald Colman. And on it goes, for some into the nineties or hundreds.

Is it worth living so long? You bet.

By keeping active and committed, you can indeed realize the truth of "the best is yet to be."

I have.

about the author

david brown, in partnership with Richard D. Zanuck, is associated with some of the more memorable films of recent times including Academy Award winner *The Sting,* which they presented, and *Jaws, The Verdict* and *Cocoon* which they produced.

The duo launched Steven Spielberg on his maiden directorial voyage in films, having produced *The Sugarland Express* and *Jaws,* Mr. Brown also served as Executive Producer for the Academy Award winning film *Driving Miss Daisy,* which Richard D. Zanuck and Lili Fini Zanuck produced.

Mr. Brown also produced the critically acclaimed and award winning Robert Altman film, *The Player,* Rob Reiner's Academy Award nominated *A Few Good Men,* starring Tom Cruise, Jack Nicholson, Demi Moore, Keifer Sutherland and Kevin Bacon, *The Saint* starring Val Kilmer and Elisabeth Shue and directed by Phillip Noyce and, with Mr. Zanuck, *Deep Impact* directed by

Mimi Leder and starring Morgan Freeman, Robert Duvall, Tea Leoni, Vanessa Redgrave, Maximilian Schell and Elijah Wood.

Mr. Brown and Joe Wizan produced *Kiss the Girls,* a thriller starring Morgan Freeman and Ashley Judd, a worldwide hit, and *Along Came a Spider,* another successful Alex Cross film starring Morgan Freeman.

Recently in release was multi-Academy Award nominated *Chocolat,* a major hit worldwide, directed by Lasse Hallstrom, starring Juliette Binoche, Johnny Depp, Judi Dench and produced by Mr. Brown, Kit Golden and Leslie Holleran. In development are Leif Enger's *Peace Like a River* and John O'Hara's *Appointment in Samarra.*

Prior to that Mr. Brown and Scott Rudin produced *Angela's Ashes* as a film for Paramount, starring Emily Watson and Robert Carlyle and directed by Alan Parker, based on the unprecedented success of Frank McCourt's Pulitzer Prize-winning memoir.

The Academy of Motion Picture Arts and Sciences on March 25, 1991, awarded Mr. Brown and Mr. Aznuck the Irving G Thalberg Memorial Award, given only by the Board of Governors of the Academy to "a creative producer whose body of work reflects a consistently high quality of motion picture production." At that time, there had only been 27 such awards given in the

Academy's 65-year history. In addition, and also with Mr Zanuck, Mr. Brown received from the Producers Guild of America the David O. Selznick Lifetime Achievement Award on March 3, 1993.

In addition, Mr. Brown has had a long career as a journalist, author and magazine editor (including having been Managing Editor of *Cosmopolitan,* (in the pre-Helen Gurley Brown years), as well as a film executive.

Mr. Zanuck and Mr. Brown headed film production for years at 20th Century-Fox and later at Warner Brothers. Mrs. Brown was Editor-in-chief at *Cosmopolitan* for 32 years and is presently Editor-in-chief of *Cosmopolitan's* 52 international editions, which she launched.

Mr. Brown's first book was the critically acclaimed *Brown's Guide to Growing Gray,* published by Delacorte in 1987. This was followed by his memoir, *Let Me Entertain You,* published by William Morrow to excellent reviews. His next best-seller was *The Rest of Your Life is the Best of Your Life,* published by Barricade Books, in 1991. He is also an occasional contributor to *The New Yorker.*

Mr. Brown was represented on Broadway as producer of *Tru, A Few Good Men* and *The Cemetery Club* and in London with *Vanilla.* Most recently, with Ernest Lehman, he produced the multi-Tony nominated musical based on the classic film *The Sweet Smell of Success* for

Broadway. John Guare wrote the book, Marvin Hamlisch composed the music, Craig Carnolia the lyrics and Nicholas Hytner directed. John Lithgow won the Tony for best actor in a musical, Brian D'Arcy James and Kelli O'Hara starred, in addition with Ben Sprecher

Mr, Brown produced the play, *Mr. Goldwyn* starring Alan King and directed by Gene Saks off Broadway and Jerry Herman's *Showtune,* which he produced with Jennifer Strome off Broadway.

On Broadway currently, produced by Mr. Brown and Marty Bell, is *Dirty Rotten Scoundrel.* It stars Jonathan Pryce, Norbert Leo Butz, who won the Tony for best actor in a musical, Sherie Rene Scott, Joanna Gleason and Gregory Jbara, directed by Jack O'Brien, book by Jeffrey Lane, music and lyrics by David Yazbek.

In preparation at this writing, also produced by Mr. Brown and Marty Bell, is Thornton Wilder's *The Skin of Our Teeth,* directed by Gabriel Barre, book by Joseph Stein, music by John Kander, lyrics by Fred Ebb.

Mr. Brown will also produce the life story of Billy Wilder, *Nobody's Perfect* by Charlotte Chandler and directed by John Tillinger.

In television, Brown and William S. Gilmore produced an award-winning series for Home Box Office entitled *Women & Men,* based on classic short stories. In

1996 Mr. Brown produced a four-hour miniseries for CBS based on Dominick Dunne's best-selling book *A Season in Purgatory,* directed by David Greene.

Mr. Brown is a resident of New York, a member of the Film Trustees Advisory Board of the Museum of Modern Art and Board of Visitors of Columbia University's Graduate School of Journalism.